Counting 1 to 10

Daniel Nunn

Raintree

Chicago, Illinois

www.capstonepub.com
Visit our website to find out more information about Heinemann-Raintree books.

To order:
☎ Phone 800-747-4992
⌨ Visit www.capstonepub.com to browse our catalog and order online.

Edited by Daniel Nunn, Rebecca Rissman, and Sian Smith
Designed by Joanna Hinton-Malivoire
Picture research by Elizabeth Alexander
Illustrations by Joanna Hinton-Malivoire
Originated by Capstone Global Library Ltd.
Production by Victoria Fitzgerald

Library of Congress Cataloging-in-Publication Data
Nunn, Daniel.
  Counting 1 to 10 / Daniel Nunn.
    p. cm.—(Math every day)
  Includes bibliographical references and index.
  ISBN 978-1-4329-5730-8 (hb)—ISBN 978-1-4329-5735-3 (pb)
  1. Counting—Juvenile literature. 2. Birthdays—Juvenile literature. I. Title.
  QA113.N866 2012
  513.2'11—dc23   2011013017

Acknowledgments
We would like to thank the following for permission to reproduce photographs: iStockphoto pp. 19 (© Stephen Patterson), 21 (© Christopher Futcher); Shutterstock pp. 4 (© Nils Z), 5 (© Fotoksa), 6 (© Hannamariah), 7 (© amrita), 8 (© silvano audisio), 8 (© Fotocrisis), 8 (© Chris Bradshaw), 8 (© pablonilo), 9 (© Beata Becla), 10 (© Louella938), 11 (© Pkruger), 12 (© Pakhnyushcha), 13 (© Gorilla), 13 (© sf2301420max), 13 (© Gorilla), 13 (© Muellek Josef), 13 (© Smit), 14 (© Lusoimages), 15 (© Viorel Sima), 16 (© Elena Schweitzer), 17 (© pr2is), 17 (© Katrina Brown), 17 (© Volodymyr Krasyuk), 17 (© Pichugin Dmitry), 17 (© Vadim Kononenko), 18 (© Beata Becla), 20 (© cynoclub), 22 (© Thomas M Perkins), 22 (© R. Gino Santa Maria), 22 (© Kayros Studio "Be Happy!"), 22 (© Karina Bakalyan), 23 (© Mr Doomits), 23 (© Johann Helgason), 23 (© chungking), 23 (© koka55), 23 (© Irbiss), 23 (© manfredxy), 23 (© luchunyu), 23 (© verchik), 23 (© Ronen), 23 (© Alice Kirichenko).

Cover photograph of grass reproduced with permission of Shutterstock (© Valerie Potapova). Cover photographs of oranges reproduced with permission of Shutterstock (© cloki, © Max Krasnov, © Valentyn Volkov, © Nattika, © Nitr, © rook76).

Every effort has been made to contact copyright holders of any material reproduced in this book. Any omissions will be rectified in subsequent printings if notice is given to the publisher.

Printed in the United States   5978

Contents

One

One yummy cupcake, sitting on a plate.

One crunchy cookie, ooh it tastes great!

Two

Two pictures hanging on the wall.

Two sunflowers that are really tall.

2

Three

Three toy cars zoom across the floor.

3

Three seashells washed
up on the shore.

Four

4

Four tasty sandwiches, cut into squares.

Four best friends,
sitting on the stairs.

Five

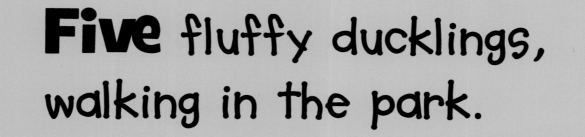

Five fluffy ducklings,
walking in the park.

Five freezing snowmen, out in the dark.

Six

Six tasty eggs, packed in a box.

6

Six smelly feet, wearing striped socks.

Seven

Seven birthday candles burning bright.

Seven parrots in a tree.
Oh, what a sight!

7

Eight

Eight coloring pencils.
Drawing can be fun!

Eight fluffy sheep, standing in the sun.

Nine

Nine dogs on a bench.
Can you count each dog?

9

Nine children running past,
going for a jog.

Ten

Ten colorful T-shirts, hanging out to dry.

10

Ten fluttering kites,
flying way up high.

Counting Challenge

How many hats can you find in this book?

Turn this page upside down to find out the answer.

Answer: There are eleven hats in this book.

Index